Welcome to Aniyah's World

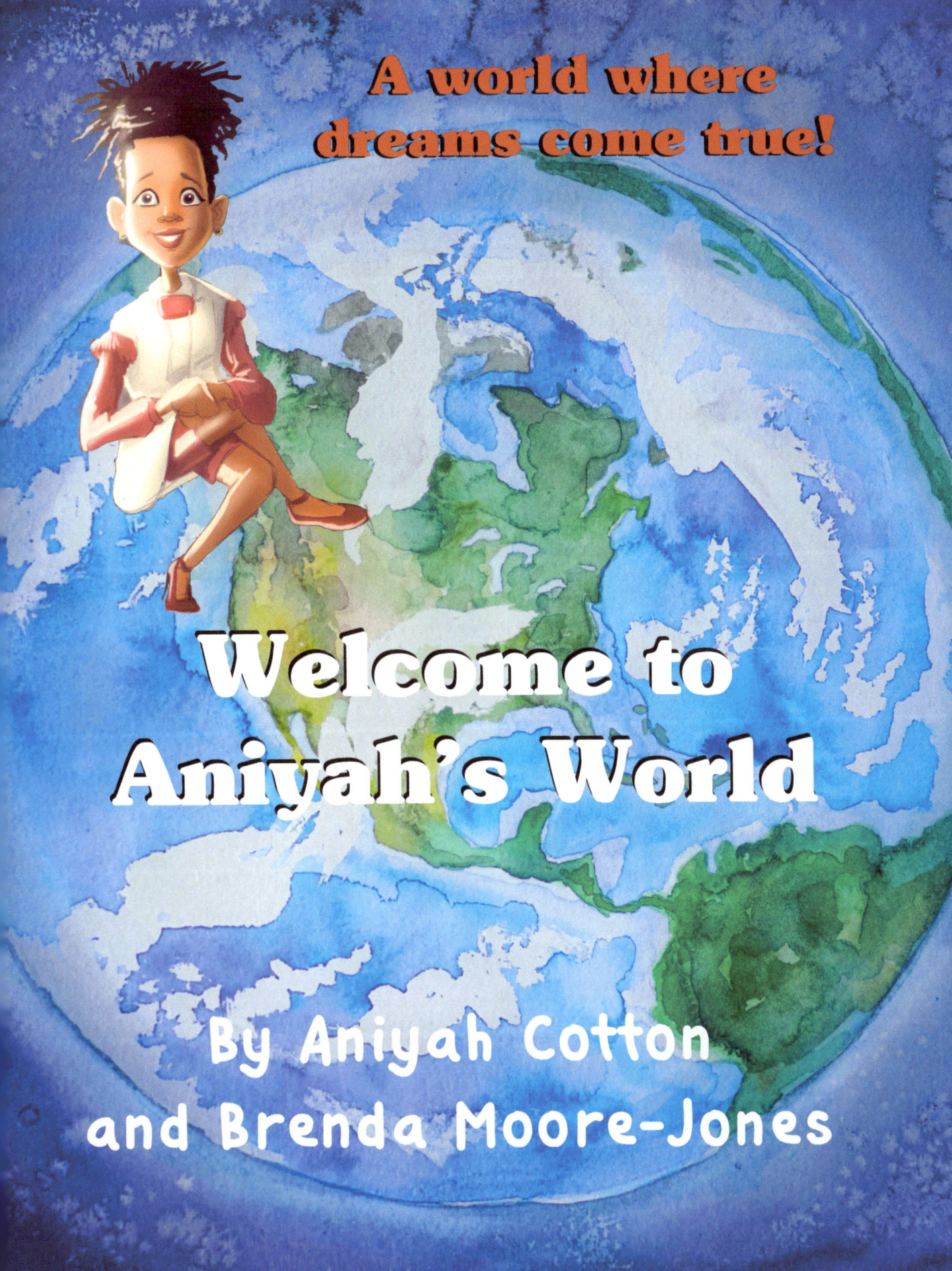

Copyright © 2020 by

Brenda Moore-Jones and Aniyah Cotton

Shena Moore-Cotton
Manager/ Booking Inquires
Cell: 833.312.3421
Shenamoore@msn.com

Brenda Moore-Jones, Assistant
Cell: 346.276.5951
moorebrenda399@gmail.com

Aniyah's World

978-0-578-82693-6

Printed in the United States of America. All rights reserved. No part of this publication may be reproduced, stored in a retrieval system, or transmitted in any form or by any means—electronically, mechanically, photocopying, recording, or any other— except for brief quotations in printed reviews, without the prior permission of the publisher.

Illustrations by Vox Illustrations
Book Production: Marvin D. Cloud

This book belongs to:

_____

From:

_____

*First, I give honor to God and I give a shout out to my mom,
my family, and my supportive grannie.
You two have helped me reach my goals as a young kid entrepreneur.
Like my mom said, "Training starts at home."
Thank you and God bless you all.*

"If you're walking down the right path and you're willing to keep walking, eventually you'll make progress."

—**Barack Obama**

When I Grow Up

You might wonder about that cutie on the previous page. That's me, Aniyah Cotton, when I was about two years old. Now I am nine years old, but people I meet, tell my mom I act mature for my age.

Some of my accomplishments are amazing. Mom tells me I have a big imagination. My grannie says, "That's good. It helps you to build character."

I love gymnastics. I am fascinated with turning flips, bending over, and cartwheels. Maybe I will become an elite gymnast, teacher, or doctor. Hmm, perhaps I can be a model or an actress. I am already a talented actress.

Mom tells me a lot, "Stop acting like a drama queen!"

I might become a great mom like her. Before I go too far, I must remember, I'm still young. My parents tell me, "You are still our little girl. Enjoy being a child."

Do you know what you want to be when you grow up?

Get your Bible out. It will guide you through life. It's time for a word from the Lord!

Train up a child in the way he should go and when he is old, he will not depart from it.

—Proverbs 22:6 (KJV)

My Future Plans

In chapter 1, I told you what I thought I wanted to be when I grow up. Mom and Grannie saw something in me, and they started me on a career path at the age of five.

Grannie said, "Only God knows the plan He has for our lives."

Well, God must have spoken to both of them about His plan for my life, because they also have big imaginations. Grannie heard about a talent search that was on its way to Houston. Oh boy! Grannie jumped on the opportunity and registered me. When we arrived at the Marriott Hotel, there were many people already there. The other contestants had a variety of talents. Some were singers and others were models or actors. A few even did comedy.

Mom and Grannie tried to explain to me why we were there, but I didn't understand. What did that have to do with me? I wanted to go to Chuck E. Cheese.

Mom asked me, "How old are you?" and "What is your date of birth?"

I thought, *she doesn't know how old I am or my date of birth?*

She explained, "Other people will come up to you and ask you those questions."

She was right; they did. I didn't know what was going on, but the longer we were there, the more fun I had.

Finally, an instructor told us to line up.

I said, "Oh, boy! We will play a game!"

I was the first one in line. The instructor pointed to the ground and explained, "I want you to walk from this point, stop over there, turn around, then strike a pose."

When I arrived at the last spot, I raised my right arm and placed two fingers across my face. I threw a peace sign and topped it off with a gangster lean. I amazed them and they laughed hard. Mom's and Grannie's faces were priceless. The instructor and others thought I was cute and funny.

I then learned a script, although I didn't know how to read. Mom read it to me and I memorized the lines in a few minutes. The instructors couldn't believe how fast I learned it. They told Mom and Grannie I was a talented little girl and I should pursue a career in acting. Grannie invested more in me after my training with Actors, Models and Talent for Christ (AMTC).

Grannie always said, "Tell me what my God can't do. God is good all the time."

Get your Bible out. It will guide you through life. It's time for a word from the Lord!

For I know the plans I have for you," declares the Lord, *"plans to prosper you and not to harm you, plans to give you hope and a future.*
—**Jeremiah 29:11**

My Grannie, the Babysitter

My brother, Christopher, aka C.J., is 11 years old. My baby sister, Kirstyn, is five years old. People know us as, "The Cotton Kids."

Grannie babysits us when our parents go to work, go on a date, or need a vacation. When they pick us up, Grannie doesn't look the same. At first, she is happy and has an enormous smile. She gives us hugs and kisses. But that changes when they come back.

When we are at her house, Grannie gives me instructions like, "Aniyah, see what your sister is doing. Don't let her run up and down those stairs."

I try to help with Kirstyn, but Grannie is right. She is a handful. When it's time for her to take a nap, Grannie and I find a quiet moment to ourselves. I ask her questions about God. Grannie says, "God loves us because He is our savior." She explained what "savior" means and other questions I have, in child-like language to help me understand who and what God is. She gave me a Bible with colorful photos. I told her, "I love God."

She said, "I do too!"

And she shared this with me, "Aniyah, the Word of God said the fastest runner doesn't always win the race, and the strongest warrior doesn't always win the battle. The wise sometimes go hungry, and the skillful are not necessarily wealthy. And those who received an education, don't always lead successful lives."

Grannie said, "Do your best, and always put God first. He knows the plans He has for your life. Sometimes people become an overnight success. Life can also lead to disappointment. But don't give up and don't give in. Hold on to God's unchanging hands. If you fall, dust yourself off, get back up on your feet and start again. Nothing beats a failure but a try. Sometimes, it takes more than one try."

I told her, "Okay Grannie, I will."

Get your Bible out. It will guide you through life. It's time for a word from the Lord!

Commit to the Lord whatever you do,
and your plans will succeed.
—Proverbs 16:13 (NIV)

School is fun When You are not in Time Out

Our morning drill is different from our night time routine. Before Dad leaves for work, he drops me, Kirstyn, and C.J., at school. Mom is too busy getting us three children ready for the day to prepare breakfast in the morning. Most of the time, we eat breakfast at school before classes start.

I love my school and all of my teachers. For me, most of the time, school is fun. In one of my classrooms, my teacher sometimes allows me to help her out with my classmates. She is thankful for my assistance.

In another classroom, it is the exact opposite. The teacher won't admit it, but she needs my help. I don't know why she won't accept it.

One day she said to me, "Aniyah Cotton, thank you, but I don't need any help. I can teach my class. Please take your seat." She sounded annoyed.

Sometimes, Grannie comes to my school before it has let out, to pick me up early. Usually, it's to take me on an audition.

One day, she came to my school, and found me in time out. Needless to say, she was not happy with me, although I was not in time out for acting up.

My teacher told her, "I'm having a problem with Aniyah staying in her seat."

I told Grannie, "I was only trying to help her with her class." I don't think she agreed with me.

Who knows? Maybe one day I will be a teacher when I grow up. Oh, boy! If I become a teacher, the first thing I will do is ban "time out." No more time out!

I don't think it is necessary. The teachers and administration may not like it, but I know the students will love it! I can see me as a teacher because my parents always talk to us about the importance of education and I would like to pass that lesson along to other children.

Dad said to us, "This is part of life and growing up."

Mom said, "One day, you will own your own company, become a talented actress, doctor, talk show host, or an athlete. Whatever you do in life, you need to finish school, go to college, and get your degree."

Well, me, my brother, and sister, have a long ways to go, but we are on the right track. Mom always tells us we must put in the work, the time, and the effort to accomplish our goals. She reminds us that her and Dad are behind us every step of the way. I thank God for my parents. They love us very much.

Like Grannie says, "God is love, and He loves us unconditional. That's in His word."

Whatever your dream or passion may be, follow it, whether early on or later in life. You can start by participating in school programs like drama. That can lead to you being a Hollywood star. By being on the basketball team, you may end up playing for the NBA. If you are a member of the debate team, you could become a teacher. What about becoming the President of the United States? How cool is that?

Dream big! Never give up on your dream. Nothing is impossible. Whatever you decide, love what you do. That also include, getting married and having kids. Be the best parent you can be, and that will make a great difference in their journey to success. Be there for them, believe in them, and cheer them on. That will make their world go around.

I know because my dad, mom, my grannie, and other family members support all my events and activities. They also support my other siblings. We have a long way to go but the road looks positive. So tell me, what are you waiting for?

Get your Bible out. It will guide you through life. It's time for a word from the Lord!

My son, if you accept my words
and store up my commands within you,
turning your ear to wisdom
and applying your heart to understanding.
—Proverbs 2:1-2 (NIV)

Getting Ready for Dinner and Homework

When it's dinner time at the Cottons' house, we wash our hands, then sit down together at the kitchen table. My parents will select one of us to say grace over the food before we eat. We learned to pray from our parents and Grannie.

After dinner, it's time to do homework. It's like preparing for an audition. Mom says we take forever to start. It takes five minutes to go to the bathroom, five minutes playing around with each other, and five minutes to get settled down. Now I help Mom a lot. I can do some of my homework without help.

About 20 minutes later, Mom will tell Dad, "It's your time."

Their faces change and they look like Grannie when they come to pick us up. I don't think they like homework either. Grannie says, "With hard work and persistence, nothing is impossible. If you have an ear to hear and you are able to listen and follow instruction, you will eventually be successful."

Get your Bible out. It will guide you through life. It's time for a word from the Lord!

And when he had said these things, he took bread, and giving thanks to God in the presence of all he broke it and began to eat.
—**Act 27: 35 (ESV)**

Always Stay Prayerful, Close Your Eyes and Believe

After we finish homework, next on the agenda is preparing for bed. We take our baths, brush our teeth, and get ready for the next day. Mom lays out our school uniforms along with our socks and shoes. I help her with my clothes. Kirstyn imitates me. I try to be a good role model. I'll be glad when she finds a way to do her own thing, or as Mom says, "her own identity."

We pray before we go to bed and when we wake up in the morning. "Will you pray with me?" I look forward to praying with you on tomorrow night as well. See you then.

Our Father in heaven, may your name be kept holy. May your Kingdom come soon. May your will be done on earth, as it is in heaven. Give us today the food we need, and forgive us our sins, as we have forgiven those who sin against us. And don't let us yield to temptation but rescue us from the evil one. **Matthew 6:9-13 (NLT)**

Hey, I got to go now, but I look forward to sharing with you the next chapter in my book. Join me on my next journey to adventure!

Get your Bible out, it will guide you through life. It's time for a word from the Lord!

I can do all things through Christ who strengthens me.
—**Philippians 4:13 (NKJV)**

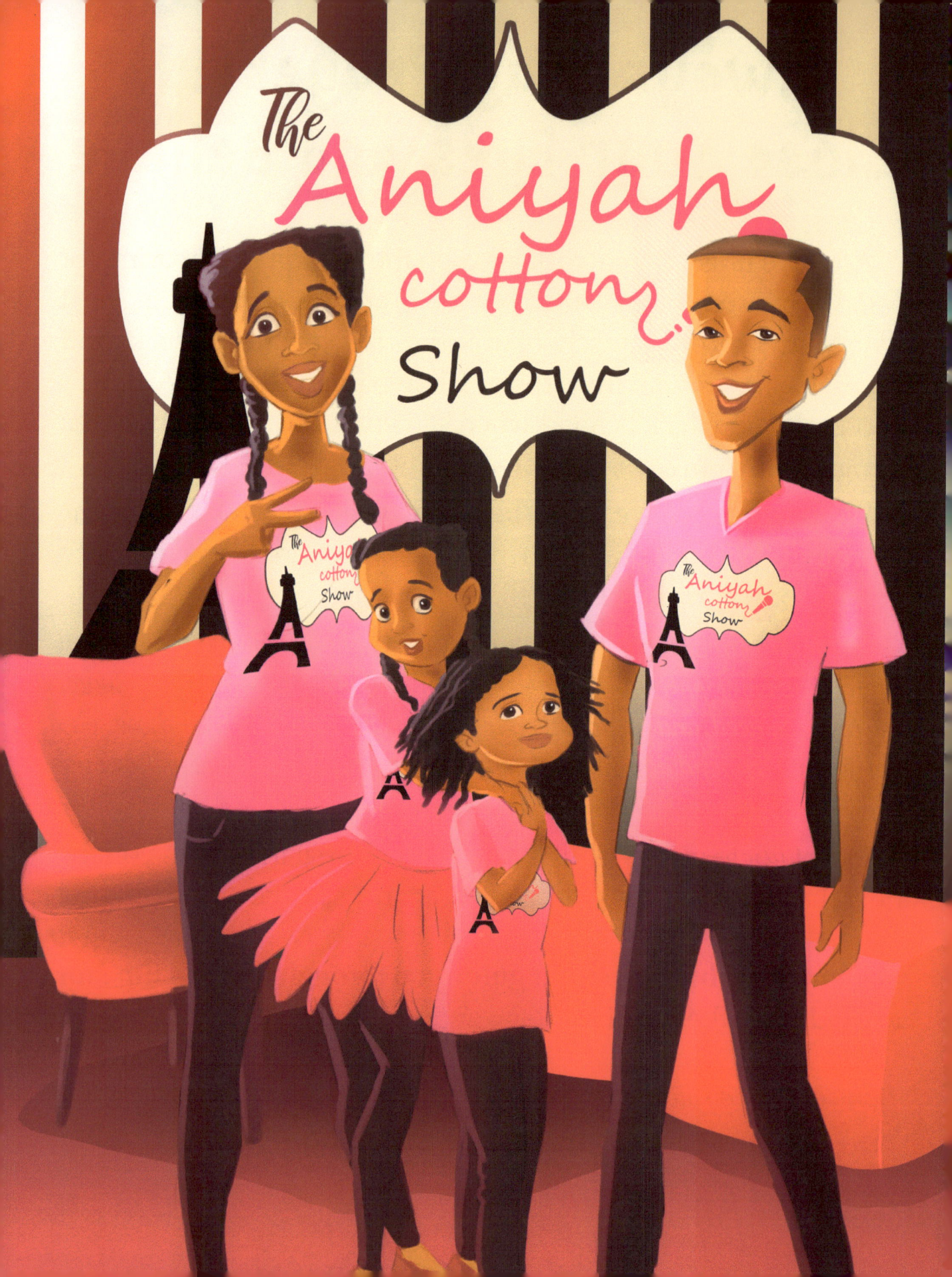

This is My Story

It all started at the age of four when Grannie and Mom signed me up with the Acting, Models and Talent for Christ (AMTC) Agency. They came to the Marriott Hotel in Houston, Texas. It was August 2, 2014. It was also my fifth birthday.

After my training with AMTC, we were on our way to Kissimmee, Florida for a competition. Me, Mom, Grannie, and Kirstyn, who at the time was about the age of one, stayed at the Gaylord Palms Resort & Convention Center. It blew away my Mom and Grannie. All they could say was, "Wow! Wow!" As we got settled in, we thought we were royalty. The hotel was like a castle. It was huge; the biggest they had ever seen.

I trained every day, and we had a lot of fun. I competed with other children in my age group and there were other age groups there with unique talents. It was amazing. If I tell you Mom and Grannie had me ready for each competition, you better believe I was ready and I was together.

Grannie said, "You are so cute from the crown of your head to the sole of your feet!"

We were there for almost two weeks. As the competition ended, they prepared me for the award ceremonies. There were judges from all around the state. There were different categories for acting. I received several awards. Mom, Grannie, and the crowd of people were proud and happy for me. A couple of guys lifted me up in the air and paraded me around the room on their shoulders while everyone else cheered me on. It was a great feeling. Acting, Models, Talent for Christ (AMTC) Agency was also proud of me because I was one of their own. Others received awards, as well. People took many photos and told Mom and Grannie I did a magnificent job. Some said they looked forward to seeing me in TV commercials.

One day I hope to be on the Disney and Nickelodeon channels, in movies, sitcoms, and working with the crew of Marvel Studios. Wow! How exciting will that be? The different talent agencies chose the best talents for their company. Some asked Mom and Grannie if they would be willing to pack up and leave Houston for New York or California? They were honored and willing to work with me. But I could tell the air went out of their sails a bit. That was something to think about. I guess Mom wasn't ready for that question. She wanted to see if there was an agency that was closer to Houston. However, being wise, she took their business cards.

An agency that was in Dallas, Texas was also there. My Mom and Grannie talked to the representative and planned to visit her in Dallas. That's who we went with, The Linicomn Agency. I'm sure it would have been tough for my parents to pick up and leave not knowing if I would make it big, but that wasn't a chance they were willing to take. Mom said it was too risky to leave behind their jobs, family, school, and start all over without a guarantee. They decided to try to commute from Houston to Dallas and the surrounding areas for auditions.

As time went on, Mom and Grannie branched out and went to other places. We traveled to California, Georgia, and Louisiana. We are still on the road to success.

Kirstyn, is an actress and she has joined me on the road. If our parents, and God are for us, who can be against us? I have been in several commercials, and an HBO movie. Not only am I an actress, but when I am not acting, I am a talk show host on the GMT 90.3 Radio, and host of the online TV program, "The Aniyah Cotton Show."

Mom got me started as a radio talk show host when I was five. I've interviewed young, talented children, and adults who are entrepreneurs, authors, actors, actresses, rappers, pastors, First Ladies, TV personalities, educators, etc.

I look forward in doing bigger and better thing as I grow in wisdom and if the Lord say the same. Like Grannie says, "He knows the plans he has for you declares the Lord, plans to prosper you and not harm you, plans to give you hope and a future," (Jeremiah 29:11). I just love my Grannie.

I was also told God will give you favor, and He will open up the windows of heaven and pour out a blessing, that there will not be room enough to receive it, according to Malachi 3: 10.

Always keep God first and take Him with you everywhere you go. Grannie said without faith, works is dead (James 2: 14-26). Keep the faith and believe with all your heart and with all your soul and might that God will guide you. His word will be a lamp unto to your feet and a light unto your path. (Psalm 119:105, ESV)

I always say, "Dream big for nothing is impossible with God," according to Luke 1:37.

As we end this chapter of my life, please go to my Social Media Page and check out on my U-Tube videos and hit the like button.

 @aniyahcotton

 aniyah cotton

 @cottonaniyah

The Aniyah Cotton Show

My fans and followers, thank you for making me what I am today by being there for me. Please keep me and my family in your prayers and I'll keep you and your family in our prayers. God bless you and remember:

Believing N 1 self is the  2 Success 1 has 2 Proceed 2 Succeed.

Never Give Up and Never Give In.
DREAM BIG! NOTHING IS IMPOSSIBLE!

www.ingramcontent.com/pod-product-compliance
Lightning Source LLC
Chambersburg PA
CBHW061400090426
42743CB00002B/92